Contents

P9-AQZ-148

What Is the Theory of Evolution?

Take a look at the plants and animals in the world around you. There are millions of different types, or **species**, of living things. Some, like flowers and dogs, we see every day; others, like bacteria and germs, are too small to see without a microscope.

↑ Some prehistoric dinosaurs were the very distant ancestors of all modern birds.

Life on Earth

Life on this planet is very diverse. There is a species of saltwater fish that has wings and can glide above the water. In Australia, the platypus has the body of a beaver, but lays eggs and has webbed feet and a bill like a duck.

Think that's amazing? There are even stranger creatures now extinct that once walked the earth. The Ankylosaurus, or "fused lizard," was armored like a tank and had a heavy club for a tail. The Brachiosaurus ("arm lizard") could grow up to 80 feet (25 m) in length—and most of that was neck!

↑ Modern birds share the hollow, air-filled bones of their dinosaur ancestors. How did this happen?

Plants and animals of the past and present share a lot of similarities, or **traits**. How is that possible? How can a bat's wing resemble a dolphin's flipper? How can a dinosaur from hundreds of millions of years ago have characteristics like those of a bird living today?

The Theory of Evolution

Billions of years ago, before the earliest human beings and even before the dinosaurs, the only living things on Earth were tiny **single-celled** organisms. Every living thing on Earth developed from these microscopic organisms. It is because of these shared ancestors that different plants and animals, both living and extinct, share so many characteristics.

The **theory** of evolution is one of the most important areas of research and study in nature. It provides an explanation for how the amazing diversity of life on Earth could come from simple single-celled organisms, and for how life forms change over time in response to their environments. It allows human beings to understand where we came from, and to shape our own future. Knowing how organisms have evolved over time has been very helpful in areas such as medicine. Viruses and other harmful **microbes** have evolved just like all living things, and scientists can use their evolutionary histories in finding cures.

→ Even single-celled organisms evolve and adapt to their environments.

Law versus Theory

A **scientific law** is a statement that describes something about how the natural world behaves under controlled circumstances. A scientific law describes what happens every time something has been tested. For example, the law of conservation of mass states that in an ordinary chemical reaction, the amount of each chemical will not change in a detectable way. A **scientific theory** is a well-supported explanation for how facts fit together. The theory of evolution, while accepted as a fact by most scientists, cannot be tested in a laboratory, so cannot be called a "law."

Darwin's Big Theories

A British naturalist and explorer named Charles Darwin (1809–1882) was fascinated with the diversity of living things. In 1832, he set sail aboard the HMS *Beagle* for a mapping expedition to South America. On his travels, Darwin observed a huge diversity of plants and animals, most famously on the Galapagos Islands.

On these islands in the Pacific Ocean, Darwin noticed many similarities among different species of birds, particularly the finches. Each of the 13 species of finch had a beak that suited its feeding habits. Darwin noticed that all 13 species of finches were related to the South American finch. On each island, the finches had evolved differently in a way that helped them survive on that particular island.

↑ *The many unique species of finches on the Galapagos Islands caused Darwin to look for a common ancestor.*

This discovery helped guide Darwin to develop his theories of natural selection and evolution. He proposed that through natural selection, evolution allowed a species to adapt and better survive in its environment. Darwin continued to observe plants, animals, and fossils, and to think about how to explain the changes in species over time, and about how new species were created. In 1859, Darwin published his theories in his book *On the Origin of Species by Means of Natural Selection, or the Preservation of Favoured Races in the Struggle for Life.*

"Seeing this gradation and diversity of structure in one small, intimately related group of birds, one might really fancy that from an original paucity of birds in this archipelago, one species had been taken and modified for different ends."

—Charles Darwin, in a comment added to the second edition of *The Voyage of the Beagle* (1845)

In the Beginning

Darwin's ideas received heavy criticism from people who accepted some of the popular theories of natural history of the time. One of these theories, called **creationism**, came from the Bible. It taught that God created all life on Earth over a period of seven days.

Theories of Evolution

Before Darwin, other scientists observed living things, and came up with their own theories of evolution based on scientific evidence. Jean-Baptiste Lamarck (1744–1829) was one of the first to suggest a natural force behind evolution. He looked at fossil records, and proposed that all living things became more complex over time. Pierre-Louis Moreau de Maupertuis (1698–1759) believed that a male and female each contributed "particles" to their offspring. Some of these "particles" were **dominant**, and were more likely to be passed on to later generations.

← *Today, the Galapagos Islands are still home to unique species, much as they were in Darwin's day.*

Taxonomy

Taxonomy is the science of classifying and naming organisms. Scientists use a classification system developed by Carl Linnaeus (1707–1778). Living things that can produce **viable** offspring are grouped into *species*. A group of species is called a **genus**. The name of the genus and species make a species' scientific name. The scientific name of the Galapagos Crab is *Grapsus grapsus*. The species name and the genus name are both *Grapsus*.

CHAPTER ONE

The facts About fossils

Fossils are the hardened remains of living things that are buried in rock underground. These remains can include bones, teeth, eggs, bits of plants, and imprints left behind by humans and animals.

Buried Pieces of the Past

Most plants and animals **decompose** after they die. Oxygen and water break down the remains over time, leaving no trace. When the remains of living things are buried under sand and dirt, especially in underwater environments, they can be preserved. Over many years, movement in Earth's crust pushes the rock up to the surface.

↑This Ursus spelaeus, or prehistoric cave bear, lived in Europe during the Pleistocene, about 45,000 years ago. Most fossils of this species have been found in caves.

The Flood

The Bible tells of a flood that covered Earth in water. Prior to the catastrophe, the story says that God told a man named Noah to build a giant boat and to fill it with a male and female **specimen** of every animal so that life could continue. This story was used in arguments to explain how fossils of ocean life ended up in mountain areas. It also was used to defend the argument against extinction.

> *"One must believe that every living thing whatsoever must change insensibly in its organization and in its form.... One must therefore never expect to find among living species all those which are found in the fossil state, and yet one may not assume that any species has really been lost or rendered extinct."*
>
> —Jean-Baptiste Lamarck, *Système des Animaux sans Vertébres* (1801)

Early Fossil Theories

By the seventeenth century, **natural historians** were discovering and cataloging early creatures such as the coil-shelled *Cenoceras*. The word "dinosaur" was first used by Richard Owen (1804–1892) to name these mazing lizards. But even though these ancient remains were identified, scholars and scientists did not agree about where they came from, and why they were found where they were.

↑ *Even the* **excrement** *from a creature millions of years ago can become fossilized. These fossilized leavings are called "coprolites."*

One popular belief was that all fossils were the remains of plants and animals that still existed. Many scientists had based their own theories about natural history on the Bible. According to the Bible, God created all living things at the same time, so each fossil must still have a living example somewhere on Earth.

Historical Footnote

Frenchman Georges Cuvier (1767–1832) was a so-called "catastrophist." Catastrophists believed Earth had been shaped dramatically by a series of **cataclysmic** events. They did not believe that everyday forces, such as erosion, could shape Earth slowly over long periods of time. A later catastrophist, Louis Agassiz (1807–1873) added Ice Ages to the list of Earth-changing calamities. He was correct about Ice Ages changing the surface of Earth; however, we now know that the changes happened very slowly over time.

Geology Explains

As scientists learned more about **geology**, they also learned more about fossils. By the 1800s it was proven that Earth's surface was built upon layers of rocks called **strata**. These layers of rock were formed over long periods of time as mud and lava flows cooled and hardened. Fossils were preserved inside the cooled mud and lava.

The layers of rock farthest underground are older than the layers close to the surface. Sometimes the layers of rock are disturbed—by earthquakes or volcanic eruptions, for example. But if the layers are not disturbed, each layer closer to Earth's **core** is older than the layer above it. Each stratum marks a different geological period. So, knowing the age of a layer helped scientists to know the age of the fossils they found in each layer. The deeper down in the strata, the more unfamiliar the fossils look. The older, much stranger-looking fossils that are deepest within the earth are less complex. The very oldest fossils are the single-celled structures of our tiny ancestors.

←The geological strata, or layers, of earth are visible in some cliffs and rock faces.

Strong Evidence

As scientists learned more about Earth's history, they began to develop theories that opposed some of the popular beliefs of the 1800s. **Sedimentary** rock takes an incredibly long time to form, much longer than the biblical flood. Also, if most of the fossils uncovered were fossils of ocean life, then why would a flood wipe those creatures out? As scientists began to understand that Earth was built up very slowly, over very long periods of time, they rejected catastrophe theories, such as those supported by George Cuvier.

The dating of strata and the discovery of fossils buried in them contradicted the belief that all life on Earth was created at the same time. The remains of massive creatures such as the triceratops were found in strata from far distant geologic periods. Discoveries such as this also went to disprove the belief that fossils were the remains of plants and animals still living somewhere on the planet and besides, no one had run into a living brontosaurus!

→ Paleontologists use Ammonites as index fossils to define and identify geological periods.

Quick fact

According to the early Christian writer Tertullian, Earth's sedimentary rocks and the fossils found in them were deposited on dry land during the flood, when the water rose, then retreated.

Dating Fossils

Scientists know how long it takes certain atoms to break down. Many of these atoms are found in bones. Scientists measure the rate of decay of these atoms in fossils to find out how old they are. Another less accurate way to date fossils is by comparing where a fossil was found to other fossils in rock. The lower you go, the older the fossils.

An Evolutionary Timeline

Scientists recorded and dated both layers of geologic strata and the fossils found in each layer. In this way, they were able to map the ways that species changed over very long periods of time. First, scientists put species that looked similar into groups. But some similarities were more difficult to notice. Lamarck was one of the first scientists to group species of living things by the structure of their internal parts, and not just by whether two organisms looked alike. His approach looked at how fossilized remains had similarities or differences in the way their bones were shaped and fit together. Grouping fossils this way helped scientists trace relationships between different species. It also allowed scientists to ask questions and **hypothesize** about an organism's environment when it was alive.

Mammal-like reptiles have provided some of the most complete fossil timelines showing evolutionary changes. Beginning almost 300 million years ago, these organisms slowly evolved into mammals during the Mesozoic **Era**, which ended around 65 million years ago. Discoveries of fossils such as the cynodont have been extremely helpful in tracking this progression from reptile to mammal.

←Bienotherium yunnanense *is a transitional species of cynodont. The skull is shaped like the skull of a mammal, but scientists think that they laid eggs like reptiles.*

n Transition

Transitional fossils, or intermediates, help scientists track the changes that an organism goes through as it evolves into a new species. Fossilized remains are rare, but intermediates are really rare. When they are found, they are very helpful to scientists in connecting later species to earlier ones.

↓This is an artist's reconstruction of Tiktaalik roseae.

Intermediates living today also play a role in understanding evolution. These creatures display in-between characteristics seen during evolutionary change. At one time scientists asked only how they could classify these creatures: is a fossil of a winged fish a fish or a bird? If a warm-blooded furry creature lays eggs, is it still a mammal? Today we know that living intermediates can help us understand the evolution of similar species in the past. Flying squirrels, who glide through the air, allow scientists to speculate on the evolution of other tree dwellers who might have evolved into flying creatures, such as bats.

Quick fact

The transitional fossil *Najash* is an early snake. It had two hind limbs.

An Important Intermediate

Finding the in-between species of organisms is very exciting for scientists. In 2006 a group of scientists discovered a creature that looked like a cross between a fish and a lizard. Named the *Tiktaalik rosae* ("large fish in a stream"), this intermediate organism lived almost 375 million years ago. It had the gills and scales of a fish, but also had a set of lungs that could breathe oxygen. The *Tiktaalik rosae*'s four fins also resembled the wrist and finger structure of other four-legged land animals.

An Incomplete Record

Fossils give us a record of some of the life on Earth from millions of years ago, but the record is not complete. We do not have fossils of every living thing that existed, so it is very rare for scientists to be able to trace all of the descendents of a prehistoric species. There just are not that many fossils, and only a small percentage of the fossilized remains that exist have been found. Some scientists estimate that of all living things that existed, as few as one percent or less have been discovered.

Considering how unlikely it is that something from millions of years ago would survive as a fossil, it is astounding that we have found as many as we have. Gaps in the chains of fossils make it difficult to trace the evolution of different species. Some people argue that these "missing pieces" disprove the theory of evolution. How can you prove an organism evolved from one species to another without showing the in-between stages?

→ *Trilobites swam in Earth's oceans during the Paleozoic era, about three million years ago. The fossil record for trilobites is larger than for many other creatures because fossils from aquatic creatures are much more common than those from land-dwelling creatures.*

As mentioned before, the forming of a fossil is incredibly unlikely, especially on land. Most plants and animals die out in the open. This leaves their remains to fa the elements, such as wind, sun, and ra as well as scavengers who feed off dea organisms. The odds are greatly in favo of the remains breaking down and returning to the Earth.

It is because of these odds that most fossils found today are of water-dwelling organisms, such as trilobites. Sand and sediment under water build up faster there than on dry land.

Work in Progress

The questions of evolution are far from being answered. Scientists still need to find intermediates between species for many of the recorded eras. The explosion of new life during the Cambrian period from over 500 million years ago marked the appearance of a huge number of relatively complex creatures. Scientists are still working to gather evidence of evolutionary ancestors for all of these creatures.

New fossil discoveries are made regularly around the world. Believe it or not, these continuing efforts create even more evolutionary questions. The more fossils found of a genus, the bigger and more complicated the list of its species becomes.

↓ Fossils of many mammals, including this unidentified horse, have been found in the La Brea Tar Pits.

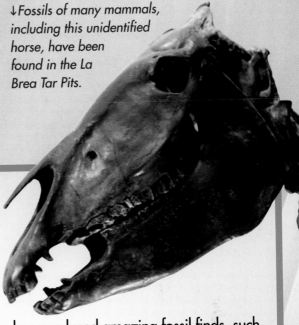

The La Brea Tar Pits

Found in Hancock Park, California, the La Brea Tar Pits have been the discovery site for millions of fossils. Named after the pools of crude oil that seep out of the ground there, La Brea has produced amazing fossil finds, such as the only complete skull of a saber toothed cat ever found. The Tar Pits hold so many fossil remains because the pools of oil could trap and keep any creature unfortunate enough to step in them. The oil also helped to preserve the remains.

CHAPTER TWO

Evolutionary Theory Takes Shape

Charles Darwin may be the leading figure of evolutionary theory, but there were many before him who tried to explain life on our planet.

Before Darwin

People have always told stories about how life began on Earth. One of the most widely believed explanations for life on our planet came from the Bible. The Bible credited God with providing the "spark of life," and creating the world and life in it in seven days. According to this belief, all living things are today as they were thousands of years ago.

Other people in the ancient world used observation to come up with theories about life on Earth. In ancient Greece, philosophers such as Aristotle (384 B.C. –322 B.C.) believed all organisms could be organized into a "ladder of life," with a living thing on each rung of the ladder. Aristotle considered human beings the highest form of life, so he put humans at the top. Each step down the ladder meant a lower, less-complex organism.

Ideas about the development of life had been around for thousands of years. This chapter will look at some of the theories that came before Darwin, some of which would have an impact on Darwin's later work.

←Even in the modern period, species go extinct. The Bulldog Rat, Rattus nativitatus, lived on Christmas Island. The last specimen was seen in 1903.

Lamarck and Adaptation

French scientist Jean-Baptiste Lamarck's theory of changes to life over time was one of the first to include a driving force behind change in nature—or two driving forces, to be precise. According to Lamarck, one of these forces was an **inherent** trait in all living things to grow and become more complex. The other force was the natural process of living things adapting to better suit their environments.

Lamarck proposed that an organism could develop characteristics that would help it survive, and pass those characteristics down to its offspring.

↓ *The Thylacinus was a carnivorous marsupial that went extinct in 1936.*

So, he believed that giraffes developed long necks to help them reach food high in the tree tops. If a giraffe stretched its neck, its offspring would also have a long neck. He also believed that no species of organism could become extinct, because all living things evolve to survive in their environments. Older species didn't die out. Instead, they all evolved into new species.

Today, we know that acquired characteristics can't be **inherited**. If a parent does a lot of exercise and becomes very strong, the parent's offspring will not be born exceptionally strong. They will have to do the same amount of exercise to acquire the trait of strength.

Quick fact

As part of the process of adaptation, Lamarck noted the existence of "subtle fluids," heat and electricity, which moved through an organism. It was these subtle fluids that helped a living thing evolve and become more complex.

In a Monk's Garden

Gregor Johann Mendel (1822–1884) was a monk and a **botanist**. In his monastery garden, Mendel conducted the experiments that earned him the title "father of genetics." Mendel had developed an interest in the theory of **inheritance** while at school, and wanted to use nature as a way to study the idea.

Mendel observed that if he crossed a tall plant with a short plant, the resulting plant would be either tall or short—not medium-height. If he crossed a plant with purple flowers and a plant with white flowers, he got a plant with purple flowers or a plant with white flowers—not a plant with light purple flowers. This is because the genes that control each trait remain independent when passed down to the next generation. Traits do not combine or blend. Instead, the dominant genes determine which traits the offspring show. If a

↑Gregor Mendel

gene is **recessive**, the trait it controls may not appear in the offspring. Mendel's findings were published in 1865 in his book, *Experiments on Hybrid Plants*.

How Old Is It?

The discovery of strata and how they could help to date Earth's history in the 1800s was a real boon to geology. Two of the men responsible for this great leap forward were William Smith (1769–1839) and Charles Lyell (1787–1875).

←William Smith

→Charles Lyell

Smith worked digging and building canals in the United Kingdom. During this time he began making several important observations about fossils and the rock he found them in. Smith realized that each layer of strata held certain fossils. All of the fossils in a layer were from the same era. He also noticed that the same fossils appeared in the same strata layer, no matter where in the country he found them.

Catastrophe theories were popular explanations for how Earth's surface might have been shaped. In response to these theories, Lyell set out to prove that Earth's formation had been a very long, slow process. He developed a way to classify strata by observing the fossils buried there. In the layers closest to the xsurface were fossils of organisms still in existence. As he dug farther down, Lyell observed fewer and fewer remains of plants and animals living today. Lyell was also the first to divide the geological **epochs**: Paleocene, Eocene, Oligocene, Miocene, and Pliocene. His discoveries helped lead to the creation of **stratigraphy**, the study of strata in relation to geologic time.

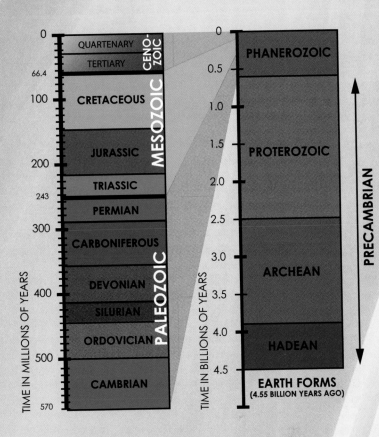

↑ Lyell identified and named the strata of the Earth. The oldest layers are the deepest, closest to Earth's core. The newest are closest to the surface. As time passes, changes happen more quickly.

Uniformitarianism

Lyell used his findings to contradict the catastrophe theory with his own theory called **Uniformitarianism**. Lyell theorized that Earth was shaped slowly over time by natural forces, such as erosion and volcanic activity. These forces have been at work since the beginning, and are still at work today.

Crowding and Competition

The **Industrial Revolution** in Britain in the late eighteenth century saw people flooding into cities from rural areas. New technologies created many new jobs in factories in the towns and cities, and many people came to do these jobs. The cities were struggling to support their growing populations, and nobody knew what to do about problems like overcrowding.

Reverend Thomas Malthus (1766–1834) was a professor of political economy and modern history. He worried about the crowded and unhealthy conditions in cities. In 1798, Malthus published "An Essay on the Principle of Population." In his essay, he proposed that a population reproduced much faster than its supply of food. When there were too many people, and not enough food, Malthus believed "natural" factors, such as disease, starvation, and war, would make the population smaller.

Finding Patterns

Etienne Geoffroy St. Hilaire (1772–1884) is remembered for his work in finding similarities in the structure of different organisms. He is also remembered for the long and heated debates he held with Cuvier, the catastrophist. Both men worked at the National Museum of Natural History in Paris, France, at the close of the French Revolution.

In his book, *Philisophie Anatomique*, published in 1818, St. Hilaire presented the theory of **homologous** structures. He believed that similar structures in different organisms, such as a human's arm and a whale's flipper, may differ in appearance, but are basically the same. These similarities would allow us to trace back lines of evolution in different species all the way to a distant common ancestor.

Quick fact

Both Charles Darwin and Alfred Wallace would read Malthus's essay and draw the same conclusions from it.

Goethe's Connections

Johann Wolfgang von Goethe (1749–1832) was a famous German writer and poet. Remembered for his plays and poems, Goethe was also keenly interested in the natural world. One of his earliest observations was of the similarities between the jaw bones of humans and other mammals and reptiles.

This helped support his theory that all living things are connected, sharing a common ancestor. In 1820, Goethe published his theories on the relation between all **vertebrates**. It was Goethe who first used the term **morphology** to describe the branch of science that looks at how organisms are constructed and the similarities between them.

↓Humans and whales seem like very different mammals. However, the human hand (top) and the flipper of a whale (bottom) share very similar structures.

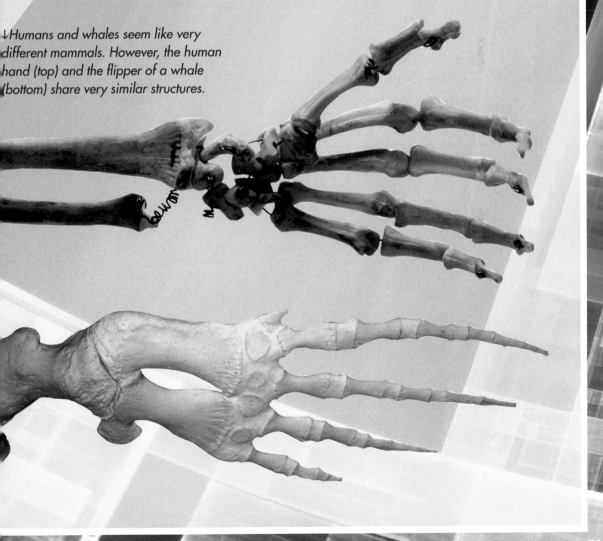

Alfred Wallace: A Distant Second

A history of the theory of evolution wouldn't be complete without mentioning a man whose own evolutionary theories were not just similar to Darwin's, but also came about at the same time. Yet, while the two men were forming their ideas, they were ignorant of each other. How's that for a coincidence?

Alfred Wallace (1823–1913) did not study science at school, but he always had a keen interest in the natural world. He even left the family business to take a journey to South America—just as Darwin did on the HMS *Beagle*. He would spend several years in South America, looking at different organisms to see if he could find similarities in their development. Wallace also wanted to find evidence that environmental factors, such as the climate or the availability of food, shaped the ways in which living things adapted.

Unfortunately for Wallace, while he did observe evidence to support his theory of evolution, he was unable to discover why some traits survive from generation to generation and others do not. Unwilling to give up on his mission, Wallace traveled to Indonesia.

Over the next few years he visited most of the major islands, collecting evidence to support his theory as well as discovering thousands of new species previously unknown to the scientific community.

"*The present geographical distribution of life upon the earth must be the result of all the previous changes, both of the earth itself and of its inhabitants.*"

—Alfred Wallace on plant and animal distribution, *Contributions to the Theory of Natural Selection, A Series of Essays*, 1871

Inspiration Strikes!

In Indonesia, it looked like Wallace would hit the same roadblock as he had in South America—until he read Malthus's essay on population. Wallace finally had an idea about survival of the fittest. His idea was that within a population, some individuals have qualities that help them survive in their environments. These individuals are likely to live longer than others who do not have the same traits. This was a tremendous breakthrough for Wallace, and he busily went about writing an essay of his findings, "On the Tendency of Varieties to Depart Indefinitely from the Original Type."

→ Traveling in Indonesia, Wallace saw many species that appeared to be adapted to their environments, such as this orangutan.

In 1858, Wallace and Darwin finally became aware of each other's work. Wallace sent his essay to Darwin, asking him to pass it on to Lyell, with whom Darwin had become friends. Reading Wallace's work, Darwin was amazed at the similarities between Wallace's observations and his own. He accepted that he and Wallace had both solved the question of evolution, and decided to present their work together at a scientific conference later that year.

Second Fiddle

During his lifetime, Wallace was showered with recognition for his contributions to the theory of evolution. He was given awards and honorary degrees, and welcomed into the highest levels of the scientific community. It was only in the decades following his death that Wallace's contributions were overshadowed by Darwin's. Some say this is because of his unwillingness to self-promote. Whatever the reason, Wallace has remained a quiet "co-discoverer" of the theory of evolution.

CHAPTER THREE

Darwin's Journey Begins

The young Charles Darwin who set sail on the HMS *Beagle* in 1823 did not seem like someone who would become a world-famous scientist. At the age of 22, Darwin was known for being a poor student who was more interested in hunting and having fun than in studying. A medical school dropout, Darwin was in the middle of a half-hearted attempt to join the **clergy** when he received a letter that would change his life.

↑ *Charles Darwin lived many years after his voyage, and spent the rest of his ilfe conducting scientific experiments.*

All Aboard the HMS *Beagle*!

The captain of the HMS *Beagle* was looking for a naturalist to join his crew on a fact-finding journey. In 1831, Darwin found himself setting sail for South America. For the next four years, the HMS *Beagle* sailed the southern hemisphere, giving Darwin a firsthand look at thousands of species of plants and animals, as well as their environments.

As Jean-Baptiste Lamarck had done years before, Darwin observed the different ways in which organisms suited their environments.

As the HMS *Beagle* traveled through the islands, Darwin recorded similarities between different species. He found that creatures and plants living on different islands shared similar characteristics. It appeared to Darwin that location and separation played an important part in the development of different species. He also noted examples of the effects of humanity on nature. Introducing a foreign organism could change an environment, he observed, and have an impact on living things already in the environment.

Finding Answers

Darwin decided early on that in order to find the answers to his questions about evolution he would have to look at both geology and living things. Darwin was familiar with Lyell and his theories of slow change over a long period of time. During his travels on the HMS *Beagle*, Darwin studied different fossils in layers of earth across the southern hemisphere. He noticed that the numbers of a species would begin to dwindle before the species became extinct. This slow disappearance seemed to support Lyell's theories.

↓ *During his time on the Galapagos Islands, Darwin noticed that species like the Galapagos tortoises seemed to be adapted to suit their unique environments.*

When the HMS *Beagle* returned to England, Darwin set about publishing his findings in his book, *The Zoology of the Voyage of the HMS Beagle*. The book described Darwin's observations during the trip. It did not mention Darwin's theory of evolution because he was still forming it. It would be almost 20 years before Darwin shared his theory with the world.

Did You Know?

Mount Darwin, in Tierra del Fuego, and the Darwin Sound are both named after Charles Darwin. Admiral Fitzroy, the captain of the HMS *Beagle*, named the mountain after Darwin on Darwin's twenty-fifth birthday. The Darwin Sound got its name after Darwin saved his shipmates from being marooned.

A Natural Process

Back in England, Darwin wasted little time getting to work on his theory of evolution. While aboard the HMS *Beagle*, Darwin had observed many similarities between different species of animals. Most famously, Darwin noted the many species of finch that had evolved on the Galapagos Islands. All the species of finch had a common ancestor back on the South American mainland. This led Darwin to believe that all organisms on Earth shared common ancestors.

Darwin understood that some species survive and others go extinct. He also knew that an environment could shape how a living thing evolves. But what was the process that caused all these variations of species? How could so many different varieties of a living thing seem to come from one **archetype**? Darwin would wrestle with these questions for some time. One day, however, he happened across an essay by Reverend Thomas Malthus—the same essay that helped Wallace on his own path of discovery. Darwin took Malthus's notion of competition and applied it to the natural world.

↑ In evolution, success comes from an organism's surviving long enough to pass its genes to its offspring.

Nature produces more living things than it can support. There are species of frogs that lay thousands of eggs. Darwin realized that nature controls the population of organisms through competition—which is why we're not overrun by giraffes and polar bears. Factors in the environment, such as how plentiful or scarce food is, or whether hungry predators are stronger or faster, act like an obstacle course for living. Organisms that can complete the obstacle course get to live and reproduce.

Did You Know?

Darwin did not actually coin the term "survival of the fittest." A philosopher named Herbert Spencer read *On the Origin of Species* and coined the term to describe competition and reproduction. Darwin used it in a later edition of *On the Origin of Species*, where he gave Spencer credit for this apt description.

On the Farm

Darwin was also familiar with another form of selection—an artificial one. **Artificial selection** is a regular practice with livestock. For centuries farmers have bred animals with favorable traits to make offspring with those traits: the fattest male pig with the fattest female, the fastest male horse with the fastest female, and so on. Observing this practice would help Darwin to explain the process of selection in nature.

Darwin saw that in this "survival of the fittest" theory, the organisms with the traits that helped them succeed would be the ones to live long enough to produce offspring. These offspring would inherit the favorable traits that had allowed their parents to survive, and perhaps reproduce and pass them on. Darwin tied this new discovery to the connection between the environment and a creature's ability to adapt to it. He proposed that these factors for change helped the creation of all the different species he had witnessed on his travels.

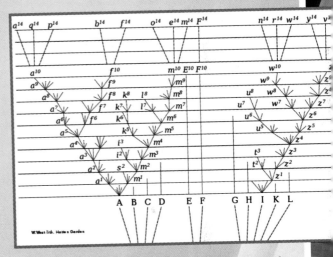

↑ Darwin envisioned the evolution of the many and varied modern species as a tree or bush, with many different branches growing from a common root.

"...It seemed to me probable that allied species were descended from a common parent. But for some years I could not conceive how each form became so excellently adapted to its habits of life...When I happened to read 'Malthus on population' the idea of natural selection flashed on me."

—Charles Darwin, from personal correspondence to Ernst Haeckel, 1864

Location, Location, Location

Throughout his travels, Darwin noted how species of the same animal, like the different species of finch or tortoise he observed, could be very different. Early in his studies, he theorized that an environment can affect an organism's development. This observation about location would help Darwin to understand the creation of new species.

Over long periods of time, an organism will evolve to better survive and multiply in its environment. If the environment changed, Darwin believed, the organism would evolve and change as well, resulting in a new species that differed from the original. Eventually, as generations pass and genetic changes continue, you can end up with an almost alien-looking creature from its ancestor.

↓←Similarities in the bone structure tell us that the modern brown bear is related to the prehistoric cave bear; this evidence also suggests that the two species occupy different branches on the bear family tree.

Quick fact

Prehistoric cave bears (*Ursus spelaeus*) lived in Europe and went extinct about 27,500 years ago.

Darwin believed similarities that scientists use to group modern species could be explained by the idea that all modern species had common ancestors. The differences, he believed, could be explained by the different environments in which different species evolved.

Let's use bears as an example. Suppose that many years ago, the closest relative to the modern bear lived in one part of the world. Now imagine that a part of the "original bear" population was separated from the rest. Faced with a new environment, with different types of food and different threats, many bears might die in the new environment. The bears that survived would be those bears that had traits that allowed them to survive—the bears that were best at finding food, for example. Slowly, over time, the population of bears would evolve to adapt to their surroundings. If their new home is colder, they may develop thick hides and fur. Depending on what is available in terms of food, characteristics like teeth and claws may change to help this population feed.

As years pass and more and more evolutionary changes take place, this new species of isolated bear will start to branch off not only in appearance and behavior, but also at a genetic level. This means that eventually, if the isolated species should ever run into its former group of bears, they would be unable to mate and produce offspring. The evolution of a new species would be complete.

By figuring out the role adaptation and environment play, Darwin was well underway in explaining the nature of evolution. Now all he had to do was figure out just *how* this process worked. Sounds simple, right?

←The modern brown bear shares an ancestor with the prehistoric cave bear; however, brown bears evolved more directly from a prehistoric species called Ursus etruscus. The oldest specimens of brown bear species are from China; the bears migrated to Europe and outcompeted Ursus spelaeus.

CHAPTER FOUR

A Reaction to Darwinism

ON

THE ORIGIN OF SPECIES

BY MEANS OF NATURAL SELECTION,

OR THE

PRESERVATION OF FAVOURED RACES IN THE STRUGGLE
FOR LIFE.

By CHARLES DARWIN, M.A.,

FELLOW OF THE ROYAL, GEOLOGICAL, LINNÆAN, ETC., SOCIETIES;
AUTHOR OF 'JOURNAL OF RESEARCHES DURING H. M. S. BEAGLE'S VOYAGE
ROUND THE WORLD.'

LONDON:
JOHN MURRAY, ALBEMARLE STREET.
1859.

The right of Translation is reserved.

↑On the Origin of Species
was not the first book to
explain ideas of evolution. But
Darwin's big book, along with
Wallace's essay, was the first to
propose natural selection and
adaptation as the ways that
species adapted and evolved
to suit their environments.

When Darwin found out about the similar work that Wallace was doing on evolution, he hurried to gather his observations and get them ready to print. His friends and colleagues encouraged and helped him and in just over a year Darwin was ready to publish his findings. Darwin's ideas were so revolutionary—not to mention a little scandalous for the time—that the first copies of *On the Origin of Species* sold out quickly. Everyone wanted to read about these exciting new ideas, both in the scientific community and the general public. Several reprintings had to be ordered to meet the growing demand for copies of Darwin's book.

At first Darwin was worried about revealing his theories. His ideas clashed with many popular scientific theories of the day. And there were still many questions about evolution he had yet to fully explain. There were also concerns about how people would react to the religious impact of Darwin's book. For centuries it had been widely accepted that the Bible's explanation for life on Earth was the only answer. Darwin knew this, and worried that he would be accused of attacking **Christianity**.

People Are Talking

Nonetheless, the book went to print. Darwin had done his best to explain the ins and outs of evolution, accepting that there were still some things he could not fully explain. Now all that remained for Darwin to do was to face a storm of public opinion, both for his work, and against it.

Almost as soon as it hit the bookshelves, *On the Origin of Species* created two very different sides of an argument. Defending Darwin were respected members of the scientific community, such as his friends Lyell and biologist Thomas Henry Huxley (1825–1895). In fact, it would be Huxley who would act on behalf of Darwin in many public debates over *On the Origin of Species*.

The "against" side of the argument had some surprising figures including Admiral Fitzroy, the captain of the HMS *Beagle*, the ship on which Darwin formed the earliest parts of his theories on evolution. Like many of Darwin's critics, Fitzroy was very religious and was offended by what he saw as attacks on his beliefs. Even one of Darwin's old teachers, professor Adam Sedgwick (1785–1873), dismissed the ideas presented in *On the Origin of Species*.

"Darwin's Bulldog"

Huxley would become one of Darwin's most vocal supporters. Darwin was a shy man by nature, and didn't want to take part in the heated public debates over his work. Huxley was an accomplished and respected scientist, and stood in for Darwin to defend his theories against critics. Huxley's devotion led to him being known as "Darwin's bulldog."

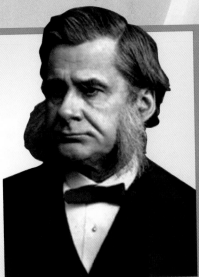

A Question of Faith

Some of Darwin's most vocal critics were from religious circles. Darwin had offended many people by trying to explain natural causes for things that they believed were caused by a **divine power**. Darwin had been careful to try not to insult anyone's beliefs. Nowhere in his book did he mention any doubt about the existence of God, but it was inevitable that his work would offend some people.

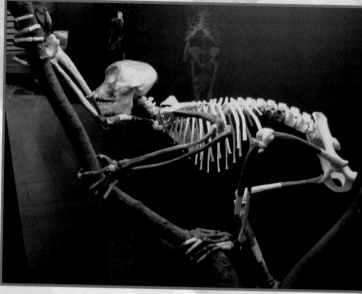

↑ Carefully examining the fossil record and the bones and physical structure of modern humans convinced Darwin and other scientists that human beings and other primates, such as this proconsul from the Miocene epoch about 20 million years ago, belonged to the same group of creatures.

The first book of the Bible, *Genesis*, tells of the creation of life on Earth. This includes how God made all life on Earth at the same time. This means that all living things, such as dinosaurs and humanity, had at some point lived together. In *On the Origin of Species*, Darwin argued that the layers of Earth in which fossils were found indicated that different organisms had lived at different times in history. The formation and dating of strata also seemed to go against the Bible's story of the Great Flood.

But perhaps the biggest problem **devout** religious people had with Darwin's work was the idea that life, particularly humanity, had evolved from less-complex organisms. The Bible says that God created man and woman, just as they are today. The idea that the human species had evolved from "lower" life forms such as early **primates** seemed not only silly, but also downright offensive.

The "Eyes" Have It

Darwin's theory of evolution depended heavily on the idea that changes happen in small ways, very slowly, over a long period of time. This idea of tiny changes and of increases in complexity brought a lot of criticism from other scientists. "How could something complex possibly come from something that was less complex?" they argued.

Darwin said that even the most complex parts of an organism come about as a result of small developments. The human eye is a very complex organ with many parts. But our eyes have evolved over time from very simple beginnings. What began many years ago as a cluster of **light-sensitive** cells like those found in worms, over time evolved to what we have today. The same evolutionary linking can be applied to all living things, showing how the birds of today are descended from giant lizards that once roamed the Earth.

An Eye for Perfection

Darwin called the human eye "perfect and complex." Simpler eyes, in organisms like crabs, Darwin called "imperfect and simple." He explained in over three pages in *On the Origin of Species* how a single nerve might develop light sensitivity, and through "numerous gradations" evolve into the human eye. He used living creatures to illustrate each stage of development.

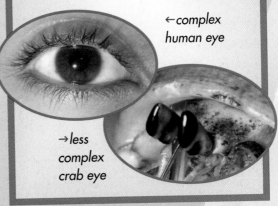

←complex human eye

→less complex crab eye

"It is an error to imagine that evolution signifies a constant tendency to increased perfection. That process undoubtedly involves a constant remodelling of the organism in adaptation to new conditions; but it depends on the nature of those conditions whether the directions of the modifications effected shall be upward or downward."

—Thomas H. Huxley

Some Questions Remain

Darwin was a pioneer. His theory of evolution was brand new, and it challenged a lot of ideas that people had. Most of Darwin's conclusions were drawn from observations. Much later, scientists would be able to use other methods to test parts of Darwin's theory, but these methods had not been invented.

Darwin was able to make a case for natural selection as the way traits survive in species but he just didn't have the knowledge to explain *how* this is done. He could only *observe* that it did seem to happen. People didn't know about genes and things like **DNA** back then. These are the **biochemical** building blocks of life, and by not knowing about them, Darwin's work was incomplete. These limitations left some gaps in Darwin's theories. The scientific community noticed these gaps, and in some cases, used them to attack his work. It would be many years before science had advanced enough to carry on from where Darwin's theories left off and complete the modern theory of evolution as we know it today.

→ *DNA in each gene carries all of the instructions to make a copy of the organism. Each strand of DNA is shaped like a tiny ladder. Each rung of the ladder is made of two chemical bases. These "base pairs" carry the instructions for making a copy of the organism.*

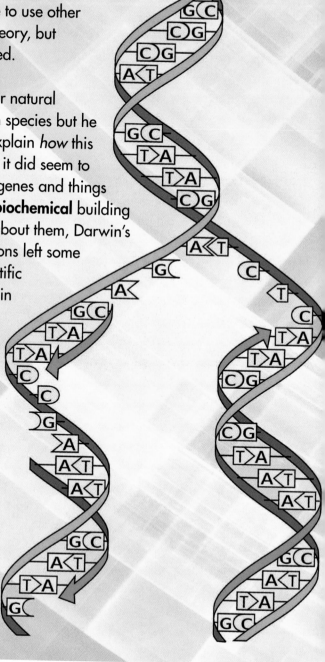

More Darwin

No one was more surprised than Darwin at the successful sales of his book. As interest in his work grew, he spent more and more time corresponding by mail with people asking questions, offering praise, and criticizing his findings. Darwin understood that there was still much work to be done on the theory of evolution. He would continue trying to explain evolution in later books, such as *The Descent of Man*, which he published in 1871.

Darwin didn't care for public debate when it came to his work. He wasn't in the best of health, and chose to answer his critics instead by gathering more information and working to improve his theories on evolution.

In *The Descent of Man*, Darwin further tried to explain the evolutionary theory in regard to humans. He would touch upon many important theories, which would continue to greatly influence evolutionary theory, such as sexual selection.

Sexual selection has to do with the traits and characteristics that attract members of the opposite sex to each other. These traits can be physical, such as the brightly colored feathers of the male peacock. They can also be in the form of behavior, such as dancing, singing, or bringing a potential mate something tasty to eat.

← *The male peacock's elaborate feathered tail makes him attractive to peahens.*

Breaking Down a Theory

"We can finally reach the solution of a question the importance of which cannot be overestimated in connection with the history of the evolution of organic forms."

—Gregor Mendel, *Experiments in Plant Hybridization*, 1865

Genetics

Darwin built his theory of evolution on keen observation and analysis. Throughout his travels, and at home, he noticed that different species are more similar when they are found closer together. He noticed that when groups of animals are separated from each other for a long time, they develop differently. He noticed that the differences between similar species were often related to the different environments in which those species lived. He observed similarities between modern species and the fossils of extinct organisms. He analyzed his observations, and found an explanation for how new species formed through natural selection. But one question remained. Darwin was able to figure out *what* natural selection is, but not *how* it happened. Darwin didn't know it, but when he was talking about variation in living things, he meant "**genetic variation**."

In Germany, Mendel's work in his garden was the starting point for understanding genetics. Through his experiments with pea plants, Mendel was able to observe and to explain how **heredity** worked. He could successfully predict which traits an organism would inherit from its parents. Like Darwin, Mendel did not have the information he needed to understand exactly why heredity worked the way it did.

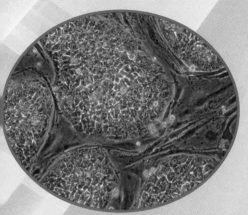

←Inside every cell of a living thing, genes carry the information that allows the cell to make copies of itself.

Genes inside every cell of every living thing are responsible for the traits, such as eye color or beak length, that get passed down from one generation to the next. Every offspring receives two copies of the gene for each trait, one gene from each parent. Each time a set of traits is passed from parents to offspring, the offspring gets a new set of genes. This means that the offspring could inherit the traits of either parent. It is more difficult to predict which trait will appear in the offspring, and the way genes appear in the next generation can seem random.

It would take many years for scientists to understand what happened inside the cells when a trait was passed from parent to offspring. By the 1920s, scientists understood that genes inside each cell enabled traits to be passed from parent to offspring. Genetics completed the theory of evolution. Darwin's theories were adjusted to include the ideas of genetics and the roles they played.

Thanks to Mendel we know that genes can be dominant or recessive. With dominant genes, the variation of the trait it creates will always appear. The traits controlled by recessive genes are less likely to show up unless the offspring receives two of that gene. This is why some of us can look nothing like our parents, but still share some of their characteristics, like intelligence or athletic ability.

←Traits, such as skin color, hair color and texture, height, and even dimples are transmitted from parent to offspring based on the dominant and recessive genes from either parent.

Three Letters That Mean So Much

DNA, or deoxyribonucleic acid, is the part of the gene that carries genetic information. The instructions for everything from the color of an organism's skin to how the organism reproduces are contained in its DNA. In 1943, scientist Oswald Avery (1887–1955) proved DNA contains the genetic code that decides how a living thing will develop.

DNA is also helpful to scientists mapping the evolution of species. For example, if two different species evolve from the same parent species, over time they will begin to have fewer and fewer similarities. The same goes for their DNA. Scientists have discovered that the number of differences in DNA between two species depends on the amount of time since they branched off from their common ancestor. So tracing the changes in the DNA is a big help to scientists who are dating the stages of evolution and classifying species. Each strand of DNA looks like a twisted ladder. When a cell reproduces, the DNA divides and makes copies of itself.

These copies contain all of the information in the parent DNA. That is how inheritable traits are passed from parents to offspring. The process is usually smooth, but on occasion something can go wrong when copies are being made—ever had an accident using a photocopier? These accidents are called **mutations**.

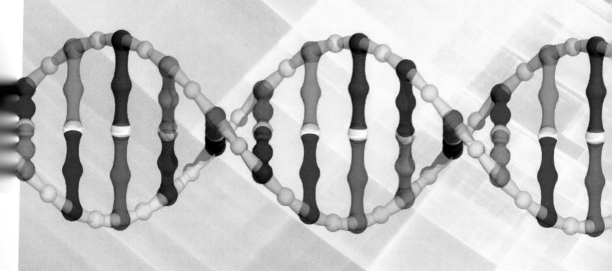

Mutations: They're Everywhere!

Mutations are what Darwin meant when he wrote about "random variations." Most mutations have no effect, either good or bad, on an organism's survival or reproduction. They simply make it different from its parents and other members of its species.

Harmful mutations are changes to the structure or growth of an organism that throw its development out of balance. The results may show up as negative changes in appearance or as physical disabilities in offspring. A harmful mutation often hurts the chances of an organism's survival, so that the organism will probably die before reproducing.

Positive variations increase an organism's chance of surviving and reproducing. For example, a genetic mutation might make an organism more attractive to potential mates, or better able to withstand disease. The changes caused by these mutations may result in the creation of a new species.

↓Drosophila melanogaster, *or the fruit fly, is one of the most commonly used organisms in biological experiments.*

Fruit Fly Facts

Since 1910, scientists have been using fruit flies to study genetics and heredity. T.H. Morgan was the first to notice fruit fly mutations. He discovered a mutant fruit fly with white eyes in a group of red-eyed flies. Scientists like fruit flies because they are inexpensive, they breed quickly, and their genes are easy to change. Perhaps most important, at the genetic level, fruit flies are similar to humans! About 70 percent of the genes and proteins found in fruit flies can also be found in humans.

Natural Selection Today

The theory of evolution through natural selection has changed since Darwin's day. For example, we now understand that natural selection can work much faster than Darwin proposed. In a study done in the Galapagos Islands (where Darwin's work began), scientists Peter and Rosemary Grant studied Darwin's finches for more than 20 years. They measured beak sizes, and observed what the finches ate, how they mated, and how many finches died. The finches on Daphne Island ate seeds that have a tough, prickly cover. After several seasons of drought, only the toughest, most prickly cactus seeds remained. Many finches that could not crack the tough, spiky seeds starved. The finches with the largest, strongest beaks survived. These finches were the most fit for the drought environment. They had more breeding seasons, and more offspring. Many of the offspring also had large, strong beaks. After the drought was over, the average size of the beak of a finch on Daphne was larger than it was before.

On the flip side, natural selection can be just as moderate as it can be dramatic. Scientists have observed that in some cases, an organism might have needs to survive that contradict each other. A small mammal might need large claws, the better with which to burrow for food and shelter. But large claws might get in the way of its ability to move quickly to avoid predators. In cases like these natural selection will most often reach a compromise. The organism will adapt in such a way as to meet both needs without hurting either one—claws that are good for digging and don't get in the way of moving.

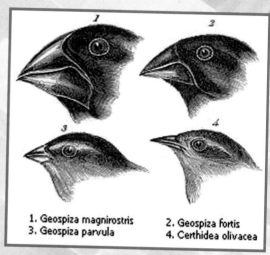

1. Geospiza magnirostris   2. Geospiza fortis
3. Geospiza parvula   4. Certhidea olivacea

"...The more you look the more you see."

—Peter Grant, *Ecology and Evolution of Darwin's Finches*

↑Darwin identified and sketched many species of finch during his voyages.

Another instance of evolution meeting survival's needs "in the middle" is when an otherwise harmful genetic trait is kept around because it also has a positive impact. Sickle cell anemia is a potentially deadly disease of the blood. But in some of the peoples of Africa, this harmful condition is continually passed along through natural selection because it can protect them from another even more deadly disease, malaria.

↑Geospiza fulginosa, *one of Darwin's finches, lives on the island of Santa Cruz in the Galapagos Islands. Different populations of this finch show different characteristics, such as different sizes and shapes of beak, depending on where they live and how they find food.*

Artificial Selection

The practice of selective breeding did not end with farmers in Darwin's day. Farmers and animal breeders have paired parents whose traits they wanted offspring to inherit. The process can be applied to plants as well as to animals. Farmers and scientists have worked to create crops that stand up better to the elements and produce more food. Because of our understanding of genetics today, artificial selection by breeders can be undertaken as early as the **embryo** stage in reproduction.

Quick fact

Natural selection is not the only mechanism for evolution. Without variation making changes in how organisms compete, nature has nothing to select.

Looking at Survival

Darwin's theory refers to life as a struggle, with organisms competing against one another for survival. Just watch any nature show and you're bound to see something faster and tougher catching and eating something slower and weaker. There are also many examples of teamwork in the natural world, such as bees working together in a hive. But even cooperation in nature is selfish. After all, bees work together in hives because their own survival depends on it.

↓ Sharks are top-level predators in their environments. They are very well adapted to their environments, and their physical forms have not changed very much (compared to those of all vertebrates and many other animals) in the past 100 million years.

When it comes to survival of the fittest, "competition" is a bit misleading. There are no winners in nature. Every organism is only the best at doing what it does. Monkeys are great at being monkeys, but they would make terrible sharks (and sharks are not at all good at swinging from trees). And everything dies and becomes food for something. Even sharks and other **top-level predators** become food for **scavengers** and **decomposers** like sea birds and bacteria.

In order to be successful in terms of natural selection, livings things just have to be good enough to survive. A kangaroo doesn't have to jump higher than any other animal. It simply has to jump fast enough to escape from predators.

The Birds and the Bees: Sexual Selection

Length of life doesn't always mean success in terms of natural selection. What matters is that the organism passes copies of its genes to the next generation—as long as it is around long enough to reproduce. It can be argued that attracting a mate is just as important as—if not more important than—surviving.

Sexual selection explains how the opposite sex of an organism is attracted to the other. As mentioned before, primary sexual characteristics (such as an organism's genitals) are directly related to reproduction. But Darwin was never able to fully explain secondary sexual characteristics, like facial hair on male humans, in his theory of natural selection. Most secondary sexual characteristics in humans and other organisms play no important role in adaptation and survival. In fact, there are species of creatures with secondary sexual characteristics that can actually hurt their chances for survival, making them considerably easier prey for predators. However, these traits are so useful in mating that they have survived in the modern species.

↑Crowned pigeons feathered "crowns" do seem to help them attract mates.

Lookin' Sharp!

There are examples of secondary sexual characteristics that can assist in survival as well as with reproduction. Some species with horns use these growths to defend themselves and their territories. Bigger horns mean a better chance at winning a fight. They can also come in handy when it comes time to choose a mate, as the females of their species base their choices on horn size.

CHAPTER SIX

Life on Earth

The earliest known life forms on Earth were single-celled organisms. These microbes floated in the oceans in the Archean eon, and stuck together in layers to form **stromatolites**. Their fossils look like dark layers of rock with bumpy contours. Over millions of years, even the single-celled life forms on Earth would become more complex.

↓Eusthenopteron *lived in the late Devonian period. Scientists used to believe that these vertebrate fish were very early four-footed creatures; however, they now know that the fish did not have legs, and lived only in the seas.*

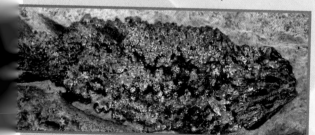

Invertebrates were next in evolutionary history. These creatures, who mostly appeared in the Cambrian perid, had soft bodies with hard shells to protect them against predators, such as a snail. They were the earliest ancestors to modern hard-shelled species like crabs. Around 400 million years ago, one of them finally grew a spine. The first vertebrates included early fish, such as Trilobites. Water-dwelling vertebrates such as fishes would become the dominant life form in Earth's oceans.

Quick fact

Stromatolites were around for a long time—the fossil record shows that they existed over four billion years. Today, stromatolites are nearly extinct. One modern species lives in Yellowstone Park.

Rock of Ages

From the types of rocks and fossils, scientists have divided the history of Earth into five main time frames: the Archean eon, the Proterozoic eon, the Paleozoic era, the Mesozoic era, and the Cenozoic era. Each marks a unique set of geologic or evolutionary events. These include earthquakes, volcanic eruptions, and ice ages.

The Big Step

The first animals to leave the water for land were vertebrates called **arthropods**. They appear in the fossil record about 530 million years ago, in the Silurian period. During this period, most of Earth's land was connected in one big landmass, that scientists call **Pangea**. Arthropods were able to make their way onto dry land using jointed legs. They breathed air with their primitive lungs, but they still had gills for breathing under water. Around 310 million years ago, some of these arthropods evolved into amphibians, who laid their eggs on land, spending even more time breathing air and out of the water. Plants also started to appear around this time.

By 225 million years ago, some amphibians had evolved into reptiles. This marks the beginning of the Mesozoic era. Reptiles would rule the planet for the next 200 million years, on land, under water, and in the air. They were not the only change to life on Earth, though.

Different species of plant life, including flowering plants, grew everywhere. But even with these strange and enormous creatures everywhere, the first mammals and birds found a way to survive and reproduce. It wouldn't be long before it was their time to rule.

The Mesozoic era ended almost 65 million years ago, and the dinosaurs went with it. Some smaller reptiles survived, and the first birds and mammals continued to evolve. Some birds would change from fliers to land dwellers. Many species of mammals began to move away from their reptile roots, growing in size and developing mammal characteristics such as fur, and reproducing by giving birth rather than by laying eggs. More and more species of mammals evolved, spreading over the planet. This period of time is known as the Cenozoic era, and has continued up to present day.

→ *Early mammals like Doedicurus were not very furry. This Pleistocene ancestor of the modern armadillo was covered in scaly skin.*

From Ape to Upright

Perhaps the most-argued evolutionary history belongs to us. In Darwin's time, the fossil record had very few examples of humanity's earliest ancestors. Evidence, such as our body structures, suggested that human beings belonged to a group of mammals that also included apes and chimpanzees. However, lacking fossils, scientists could not create an unbroken chain from the earliest primate ancestors to modern humans. Critics used these "missing links" in attempts to discredit his theory. Since then, fossil remains of humanity's earliest genetic ancestors have been uncovered, some of them millions of years old.

Quick fact

Primates are mammals that include lemurs, monkeys, apes, and humans. They all have hands and all have eyes in the front of their heads.

Branching off from other primates about six million years ago, the **hominids**, including our closest ancestors, had bigger brains than other primates. They were also the first in our line to walk upright, which helped them see a greater distance to avoid predators. From there came the *homo* genus, which was the first appearance of true human characteristics. This included *Homo habilis* ("handy man"), then *Homo erectus* ("upright man"). *Homo erectus* was the first to live in caves and wear clothes. These ancestors of modern humans could grow to about five feet (1.5 m) tall, and had dark skin.

Our species of homonid, *Homo sapiens* ("knowing man") evolved around 400,000 years ago. It wouldn't be until almost 35,000 years ago that the first modern human, the *Cro-Magnon*, appeared. These people bore the strongest resemblance to us today, with the same-sized brain and similar facial structure. *Cro-Magnon* people are responsible for the first recorded examples of prehistoric art, such as cave paintings.

"Isolated teeth, single bones, fragments of skulls: for the most part, these are the clues from which the story of human prehistory must be reconstructed."

—Richard Leakey, *The Origin of Humankind*

The Cradle of Humanity

Africa is the second-largest continent on Earth, taking up almost 12 million square miles (about 31 million km²). It has long been one of the most active places on the planet for fossil discoveries, especially discoveries of early ancestors of humans. Most experts agree that Africa is where the human species was born.

The remains of one of our earliest ancestors, *Australopithecus*, have been found in northeastern Ethiopia. These fossils have been dated at almost three million years old. The first remains were discovered in 1974. This famous find would be nicknamed "Lucy." Lucy would help provide researchers with a tremendous amount of insight into our earliest ancestors' evolution into **bipeds**.

Going even farther back is *Ardipithecus*, who scientists believe lived in Africa over four million years ago. This nearly intact skeleton took many years to carefully remove from the ground. Even older than this, *Sahelanthropus tschadensis* is estimated to have lived almost seven million years ago. It is one of the oldest known species in human evolutionary history.

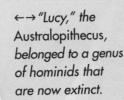

←→ *"Lucy," the Australopithecus, belonged to a genus of hominids that are now extinct.*

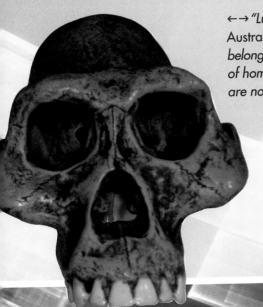

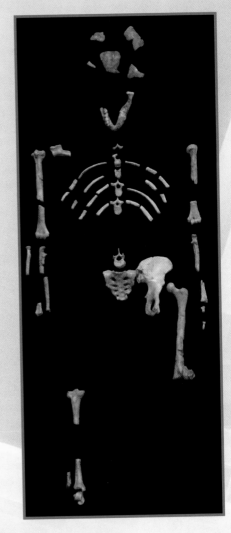

Is That It?

Human beings are a complicated species. So the evolution of the species has taken a long time and involved many changes. The species has developed from simple mammal-like creatures the size of rats fighting to survive, to complicated bipeds who have treated diseases, visited the moon, and built huge cities. With all of these developments, you might wonder: what's next?

↑ Humanity's ability to control its environment makes the species less vulnerable to threats than many other species. Does that mean we have stopped evolving?

Fossil records show that the last "big leap" in human development happened hundreds of thousands of years ago. Looking around today, it would seem our evolutionary journey has come to a halt. There are several popular theories as to why human evolution has slowed to a crawl. One reason could be our ability to live almost anywhere. From the coldest poles to the harshest deserts, people can call almost any environment home. Humans, particularly those in developed nations, possess a flexibility when it comes to different environments that no other species has. Cold? Put on a sweater. Too warm? Turn up the air conditioning. Hungry? We know how to preserve and store food. Our homes protect us from the elements. We are good at traveling: we use vehicles and go from place to place. The way most humans live today means that our bodies do not need to adapt to the environment. We use our brains to change our environments.

Or Is It?

Even with the way we live today, there still might be a call for humans to adapt to the world around us. We may be able to control the temperature, avoid bad weather, and fill our stomachs with relative ease, but there are still some things in nature that are beyond our control. These factors may call for further evolution in our species if we are to survive.

↓ We have developed vaccines that protect us from many diseases. Yet not everyone is healthy, and new diseases develop. Bacteria and viruses evolve, like all living things do.

Disease is one possible trigger for new evolutionary changes to human beings. The bubonic plague epidemic of the mid-1300s killed many people in Europe, including almost half of England in just a few months. Natural immunities to this terrible disease saved many lives. The same can be said for other diseases, such as measles.

But like all living things, diseases and bacteria can evolve to survive. In order to survive in the past, members of our species have evolved to protect themselves from certain illnesses. The time may come again when our survival depends on our natural ability to fend off disease.

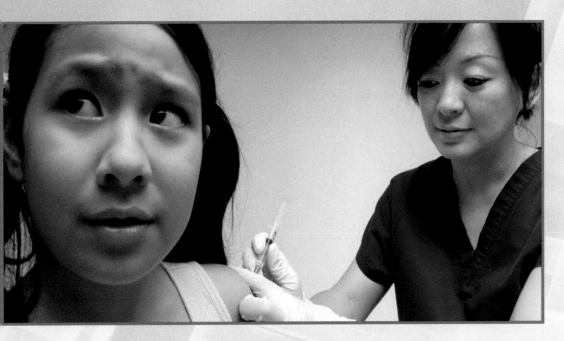

CHAPTER SEVEN

What's New in Evolution

What does the future hold for evolution? Will species of the future be even stranger and more amazing than what came before? What about the theory of evolution itself? Is there another theory somewhere on the horizon that better explains life on our planet?

A Better Tomato

Animal breeders of 100 years ago—or even 50 years—would be shocked to see how far we have come with artificial selection. In Darwin's day, breeders might **selectively** pair creatures or breed plants and crops for better results. Those days are long past. Now we can manipulate traits at the genetic level.

Genetic engineering is the changing of an organism's genes. It can take place in anything from salmon to celery. Early genetic engineering helped us do things like grow vegetables that could better survive the elements and pests. Now, thanks to advancements in the field of genetics, we can do much, much more. One of the earlier projects for modern genetic engineering was to build a better tomato.

→ *Tomatoes were one of the first foods to undergo modern controlled genetic changes. Now, it can be difficult to find foods that have not been genetically modified.*

Tomato farmers and supermarkets were tired of their product rotting too soon on the shelf. This of course was a big turnoff for customers. In the 1990s, a company in the United States set about "improving" the physical characteristics of tomatoes by changing their genetic makeup. They were able to find the gene that was responsible for the vegetable's ripening process. Through genetic engineering, scientists were able to slow down this gene, allowing the tomato to last longer before beginning to decompose.

In 1997, the government approved the new tomato for sale to the public. This was quite an event, and resulted in a lot of television and newspaper attention. As with any scientific advancement, there were those in favor of it, and those against. Most people weren't worried, because the new tomato was promised to have no harmful effects when eaten. Those against the new tomatoes feared that, because this was still a relatively new process, the genetic modification of foods might have some dangerous results we wouldn't know about until much later.

Regardless of the argument, the "better tomato" was short-lived. It turned out that by making genetic changes to the vegetable, the tomato was now more easily bruised—and no one wants to buy beat-up looking produce, right? Special transportation was needed to make sure the tomato wouldn't get damaged on the trip from the farm to the supermarket. This proved to be too expensive, and the first genetically modified tomato was abandoned.

The Food We Eat

Tomatoes aren't the only vegetable to get a "tune-up" from genetic engineers. A growing number of the foods we eat are being changed at the genetic level. Soy beans, corn, cabbage, and lettuce are just a few of the vegetables that scientists are working on. Even the animals we use for foods, such as dairy, beef, fish, and poultry, are able to be genetically modified.

Animals and plants can be made bigger, to look more appealing, and last longer. Advancements in genetic engineering have also allowed scientists to make them better for us as well. The number of **vitamins** and other healthy elements can be increased in a food. Also, scientists have found a way to produce food that contains vaccines against many diseases. For example, there are potatoes being genetically engineered to contain **antigens** that help protect against hepatitis B.

Genetic engineering has also led to new vaccines and treatments for illnesses, and, in some cases, changed how we make familiar medicines. For many years, people with diabetes relied on insulin from pigs. But thanks to genetic engineering, we can now produce insulin through modified **microorganisms**. This makes synthetic insulin much safer and easier to make.

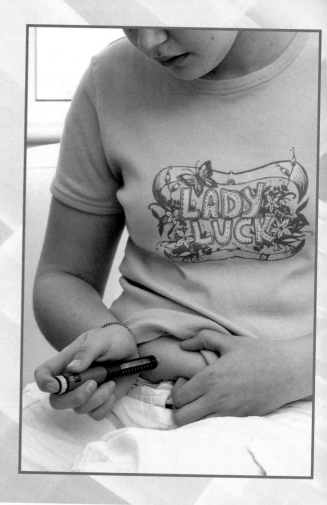

→ Manipulating the genes of single-celled organisms has allowed scientists to produce synthetic insulin much more safely and inexpensively than the previous method.

Mapping Our Genes

Some of the newest—and arguably most important—developments in genetic engineering are the ones that let human beings affect their own genetic makeup. What we know today about the building blocks of life has given us the potential to take human evolution into our own hands.

The Human Genome Project worked to identify all of the genes in human DNA. The project took almost 13 years to complete, with help from several countries including the United States, United Kingdom, China, and Japan. The **genome** is a set of chromosomes inside a cell. It contains all of an organism's genetic information. By mapping all of the genes contained inside human DNA, scientists have the information needed for helpful medical procedures.

Makin' Copies

Our understanding of genetics has also made for another fascinating advancement—cloning! Scientists have proven it possible to duplicate the DNA of an organism. This can be used to create an exact copy, using only a single cell. One of the earliest successes in cloning was a sheep named Dolly, in 1997. The cloning of humans is still against the law in most countries, but scientists continue to conduct experiments to further research on the process.

Quick fact

There are approximately 20,000–25,000 genes in human DNA, and three billion chemical base pairs.

→ Dolly the sheep was one of the first mammals cloned from cells from adult mammals. Dolly was born in 1997, and lived for six years.

To Our Health!

It has been proven that most disease is related to genes. Genetic testing allows doctors to examine a patient's DNA to see if the patient has any genetic **predispositions** for illnesses such as cancer or tuberculosis. If we know what our predispositions might be, we can pay attention and perhaps treat illnesses early.

Gene therapy is used to treat defective genes in a person. It involves taking healthy, normal genes from one cell and using them to replace unhealthy genes in another cell. Gene therapy can also be used to repair bad genes, getting them to behave normally again.

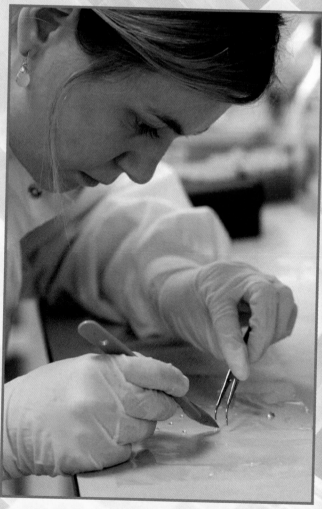

↑ Scientists use electrophoresis gel to separate different pieces of DNA. This allows the scientists to identify, classify, and sometimes make changes to DNA.

Gene therapy is still in its earliest stages of development. There are many obstacles to overcome before it can be used. One of the biggest obstacles is getting a patient's body to accept the new genes that doctors are using for treatment. Our bodies are protected by an **immune system**, which evolved to keep us healthy. The immune system stores information about disease, and attacks unfamiliar things that might be harmful. Gene therapy has the potential to treat a number of diseases, including Parkinson's and Muscular Dystrophy. One of the latest discoveries in gene therapy is that it has shown its potential for being used to treat mental illnesses, such as **depression**.

Designer Genes

Genetic engineering can help make some sick people healthy. Someday, though, scientists believe it may be able to simply create healthy people. Changing people's DNA before they are even born might allow doctors and scientists to get rid of unfavorable traits, such as the ones controlling hereditary diseases. Not only that, it could be possible to even add helpful genes, such as genes for strong bones, to a person before he or she is born. Imagine what that would be like: a pair of prospective parents meeting with their doctor, looking at a "menu" of traits their child-to-be could have. They could pick and choose the color of their child's hair, height, even characteristics like intelligence and athletic ability. This may seem a little far-fetched, but many scientists think such a future isn't that far from becoming a reality.

...There is our fascination with an evolving understanding of these amazing molecules [DNA] ...nevertheless, we are all aware that such experiments raise moral and ethical issues because of the potential hazards."
—Maxine Singer, *New Scientist*, June 1977

The Fountain of Youth

Scientists believe they may have found a way to push back the aging process in humans. We grow and heal by the division of cells. As we get older, this process slows down, finally stopping after we die. Some scientists think this is the reason why humans age, and that by extending the life of our cells, we can extend how long we live.

Meet "Ida"

Genetics aren't the only part of evolution causing excitement among scientists. Fossil discoveries continue to shed new light on the history of evolution. Most recent is the announcement of *Darwinius masillae*, or as she is called in the scientific community, "Ida."

First discovered in Germany in 1983, Ida would remain under wraps until 2009. Ida is believed to have lived over 47 million years ago. Perhaps almost as impressive is that this ancient fossil was unearthed almost completely intact, with over 90 percent of her remains recovered. She was so well preserved in fact, that the fossilized remains of her last meal were also found—fruits and leaves.

Some scientists believe Ida, whose body resembles that of a **lemur**, is one of the earliest ancestors of the human species. They propose that Ida comes from a time when our later primate ancestors began to evolve away from earlier smaller mammals. There are those in the scientific community who argue that Ida is not one of our ancestors, and is in fact just a distant relative of lemurs.

↑ "Ida," the only specimen of Darwinius masillae, was kept hidden while scientists studied her. She was originally identified as a possibly transitional species from the prosimian (pre-monkey-like) to the simian (monkey-like) primates. However, scientists are still studying and debating how to classify this well-preserved, unique specimen.

Quick fact

Paleontologists often name their finds after people. Ida is named after the daughter of one of the members of the scientific team that studied her.

Evolution's Oldest Friend

The debate between creationists and the champions of theory of evolution continued on long after the publication of *The Origin of Species*. Within the scientific community the theory of evolution became widely accepted. However, many people outside the scientific community had a difficult time accepting some of its conclusions. Those conclusions did not fit well with the teachings of the Bible, or with what people believed about humanity.

Disagreements over evolution eventually spilled over into education. Many schools in the United States have resisted the teaching of evolution in the classroom, choosing to stay with the long-held belief in creationism. In 1925, Tennessee teacher John Thomas Scopes was arrested for bringing Darwin's theory into the classroom. State law forbade teaching evolution in its schools, and in what became known as the "Monkey Trial," Scopes was found guilty of teaching evolution. Tennessee would keep its law against teaching evolution in school for the next 30 years until it was dropped in 1967.

Tennessee is not the only state with a history of problems with evolution. Louisiana had a law that made it illegal to teach evolution without teaching creationism until 1987. And in 1999, the state of Kansas removed evolution from its high school **curriculum**. Today there are still schools that prefer creationism over evolution to explain life on Earth. A kind of compromise of the two ideas, called "intelligent design," has grown in popularity over the years. In this theory, evolution is believed to have happened, but that the driving force behind it was an "intelligent cause." As evidence, it argues that complex organisms couldn't have developed without guidance.

"Nothing in biology makes sense except in the light of evolution."
—Theodosius Dobzhansky, 1973

Timeline

1798 Thomas Malthus publishes "An Essay on Population."

1800 William Smith begins his work mapping the different layers of strata.

1802 Jean-Baptiste Lamarck publishes his theories on evolution.

1817 George Cuvier publishes *The Animal Kingdom*.

1830 Charles Lyell publishes *Principles of Geology*.

1831 Charles Darwin leaves aboard the HMS *Beagle*.

1838 Darwin begins to form his theory of natural selection.

1854 Alfred Wallace leaves for South America.

1858 The works of Darwin and Wallace are presented at a scientific convention.

1859 Darwin publishes *On the Origin of Species*.

1865 Gregor Mendel reveals his studies of heredity.

1871 Darwin publishes *The Descent of Man*.

1882 Charles Darwin dies.

1925 High school teacher John Scopes is arrested for teaching evolution in Tennessee.

1943 Oswald Avery discovers that DNA holds genetic information.

1968 The U.S. Supreme Court rules that laws that prohibit teaching evolution in schools are unconstitutional.

1972 Alick Walker theorizes that birds and crocodiles share a common ancestor.

1974 Lucy the *Australopithecus* is discovered.

1977 Walter Gilbert and Frederick Sanger discover a new way to decode DNA.

1997 Dolly the sheep is cloned.

2009 The world learns of "Ida," who may be one of humanity's earliest ancestors.

Glossary

antigens Something put into our bodies that activates our immune system

archetype The original form or model from which something develops

arthropod A group of invertebrates with an external skeleton, such as crabs

artificial selection The breeding of animals to produce offspring with desirable traits

biochemical The processes that take place within living things, such as brain activity

biped A living thing that uses two legs for walking

botanist A scientist who studies plants

cataclysmic A terrible event in nature

Christianity The religion that most people in Europe and many people of European heritage in North America practiced in Darwin's day

clergy Men and women who work for a religious group, such as priests

core The center of something

creationism The belief that the universe was created by God

curriculum The different subjects taught to students

decompose When the dead body of an organism decays

decomposer An organism that helps decompose the remains of a dead organism

depression A mental illness which leaves a person feeling sad and hopeless

devout Having a great commitment to something

divine power A god or goddess

DNA Deoxyribonucleic acid, which contains genetic information for organisms

dominant Traits that are passed to offspring even when inherited from only one parent

embryo A living thing in a very early stage of development before being born

epoch A section of geologic time

era A division of time. In geology, eras are usually divided into two or more periods.

excrement Waste that is produced by the internal organs of a living thing

fossils The hardened remains of organisms found in rock

gene therapy The use of healthy genes to replace or repair unhealthy genes

genetic engineering Changing the genetic material of an organism

genetic variation The number of different genes within a population of living things

genome The set of genes in a living thing

genus A group of living things that share characteristics or traits

geology The study of Earth's physical features, such as the surface of the planet

heredity The passing of traits from parents to offspring

hominid A primate from a group of organisms that includes humans

homologous Having similar physical characteristics

hypothesize To propose an explanation for something

immune system An organism's internal process that protects it from disease and infection

Industrial Revolution A time of great mechanical developments in Britain beginning in the late 1800s

inherent A permanent and important part of something

inherit To receive a trait or characteristic from a parent

inheritance Something that is passed along from parent to offspring

invertebrate An organism without a backbone, such as a slug

law A rule that is widely accepted and followed

lemur A tree-dwelling primate with a long tail

light-sensitive Able to detect light

microbe A microorganism that can cause sickness and disease

microorganisms Extremely small organisms that can't be seen by the naked eye

morphology The study of the structure of living things

mutation The changing of a gene in an organism that can be passed down to its offspring

natural historian (naturalist) A scientist who studies the history of the natural world

Pangea A giant landmass that included most of Earth's continents

predisposition An increased chance for something

primate A member of the primate genus, which includes lemurs, apes, and humans

recessive Traits that appear in offspring only when inherited from each parent

scavenger Living things that feed on the remains of other organisms

scientific law see law

scientific theory see theory

sedimentary Rock that has formed over time from dirt and soil

selectively Chosen specifically

single-celled An organism that is made up of only one cell

species Groups of organisms that are able to breed with each other

specimens Samples taken from the natural world to be used for study

strata The different layers of rock underground

stratigraphy The study of strata

stromatolites The build-up of tiny bacteria

taxonomy The science of grouping and naming things

theory A possible explanation for something

top-level predator An organism that preys on other organisms and is at the top of its food chain

trait A characteristic

Uniformitarianism The belief that Earth's surface was shaped by natural processes over long periods of time

vertebrate An organism with a backbone, such as humans

viable Capable of producing offspring

vitamin Organic substances that help living things grow and stay healthy

For More Information

Books

Arato, Rona. **Fossils: Clues to Ancient Life.** Crabtree Publishing, 2005.

Hodge, Russ and Nadia Rosenthal. **Evolution: The History of Life on Earth.** Facts on File, 2009.

Jefferis, David. **The Earth: Our Home Planet.** Crabtree Publishing, 2008.

Lawson, Kristan. **Darwin and Evolution for Kids: His Life and Ideas with 21 Activities.** Chicago Review Press, 2003.

Silverstein, Alan, Virginia Silverstein and Laura Silverstein-Nunn. **Adaptation.** Twenty-First Century Books, 2007.

Websites

Becoming Human   **www.becominghuman.org**
An interactive multimedia project containing current research and information about human evolution

The Complete Work of Charles Darwin Online   **http://darwin-online.org.uk**
Everything Charles Darwin ever wrote, including published works, manuscripts, and diaries

The Paleontology Portal   **www.paleoportal.org**
Information and links about paleontology, including a fossil gallery and interviews with paleontologists

The Tree of Life Web Project   **www.tolweb.org/tree**
A collaborative project: biologists and nature lovers from all over the world have provided information about different groups of organisms

Understanding Evolution   **http://evolution.berkeley.edu/evolibrary/home.php**
Tons of information about evolution, including how it works, how it affects us, what the evidence is, and how the theories have developed

Index